quail studio

Published by Stackpole Books
An imprint of The Rowman & Littlefield Publishing Group, Inc.,
4501 Forbes Blvd., Lanham, MD 20706
www.rowman.com

Distributed by
NATIONAL BOOK NETWORK
800-462-6420

Library of Congress Cataloging-in-Publication
Data Available
ISBN 9780811736503

Art Editor: Georgina Brant
Graphic Design: Quail Studio
Photography: Jesse Wild
Creative Director: Darren Brant
Yarn Support: Rowan Yarns
Designer: Dee Hardwicke

British Library Cataloguing in Publication Data
A catalogue record for this book is available from the British Library

Printed in the United Kingdom

knit your story
IN YARN

First Published in 2016 by
Quail Publishing Limited in collaboration with Dee Hardwicke

STACKPOLE
BOOKS

Guilford, Connecticut

Contents

Introduction

As an artist and knitter I've always taken inspiration from the natural world and the beauty of the British countryside. I love the flowers and foliage that each season brings and the memories that they evoke. Flowers are so symbolic and they're intertwined with life's most special occasions, from weddings and christenings to idyllic summer afternoons spent making daisy chains. Their beauty is ethereal and I love to record every tiny detail of favorite plants and flowers in my sketchbooks before incorporating them into my designs. Since I've always loved the tradition of American quilts and the stories they tell, it seemed a natural progression to turn these designs into my version of a patchwork quilt that celebrates life's special memories and can be treasured for years to come.

The intarsia knitting technique is a wonderfully versatile way of translating images into richly colored knitted motifs and it's perfect for creating knitted pictures, whether you're quilt-making or planning a smaller project such as a bag, a coin purse or a set of decorative buttons. When working in intarsia you have the freedom to use as few as two colors or as many colors as your design requires so you can be incredibly creative.

I'm passionate about making the design process accessible to knitters, and this passion has developed into a series of creative Design Intarsia workshops.

Many of the people who attend my workshops start out by thinking that unless you're an artist or you understand the complexities of color theory you can't create a successful original design. It's lovely to see their confidence blossom when I reassure them that, as knitters, they're already creative. All they need is some inspiration and a little guidance to help them develop their own designs and to realize their creative potential.

In this book, I'll take you through the process of designing and knitting an intarsia heirloom quilt (I've always loved the tradition of American quilts and the stories they tell) as well as several other beautiful projects to treasure and enjoy for years to come, including a wonderfully elegant shawl, a brooch and some celebratory bunting.

I hope this book will inspire you to create your own beautiful motifs based on your favorite plants and flowers. As you journey through the book and walk through the seasons with me, knitting as you go, I hope you'll gain the confidence and techniques needed to create your very own intarsia designs to pass down through the generations.

Dee Hardwicke

Working Intarsia

The intarsia technique is used to create pictures with yarn. As an artist and knitter, I love this technique, as it works beautifully for translating my paintings and designs into richly colored knitted motifs. When working in intarsia you've the freedom to use as few as two colors, or as many colors as your design needs.

When you come to change color you just need to make sure that you secure the old yarn, the yarn that you're knitting with, with the new yarn, the yarn you're about to pick up. Securing the old yarn with the new yarn will avoid any unwanted holes in your intarsia design.

When you come to a new color on your chart, the yarn you're knitting with becomes your old yarn and the one you're picking up is your new yarn. Put the old yarn over the new yarn that you're about to pick up and pick up the new yarn from underneath the old yarn - you've now captured the old yarn with the new yarn eliminating the possibility of a hole.

Whether you're working on a right side or a wrong side row, the technique is the same for both. Just remember, "old over new."

Note

As long as the new yarn is in front of you, follow this technique. If you've worked beyond the new color and you're picking it up from stitches behind you, you can just pick up the yarn and work with it.

In this book I mainly use the intarsia technique, however depending on your design, it isn't always practical to make a butterfly (see page 19) for each yarn change. If you only have one, two or three stitches to knit in a color you don't need to make another butterfly for the existing color when you come to the end of those few stitches. Pick up the yarn from behind the few stitches you've just knitted, strand the yarn across those stitches and carry on knitting.

When you're knitting a design that has a lot of small flowers or leaves like the snowdrops in the winter section, you can strand the yarn across the whole motif. Just remember to pick up or capture your background color yarn every two or three stitches. Do this in the same way as you capture the yarn for the intarsia technique.

Reading a color chart

When reading a color chart, you need to read from the bottom right hand corner of the chart. You'll read the chart from right to left for a right side row and from left to right for a wrong side row.

Example Intarsia Chart

Working with multiple colors

When working with multiple colors your yarn will get tangled. Don't worry about this, just untangle your butterflies every so often to make them easier to work with.

Making Yarn Butterflies

Making "butterflies" or mini, center-pull skeins that won't unravel when you're knitting, is really helpful when you're working in intarsia. Storing yarn in butterflies also makes it very easy to create your favorite palettes since you can lay different butterflies alongside each other and instantly see how the colors work together. Once you've decided on the perfect scheme for a particular project, use watercolors, colored pencils or felt tip pens to record the palette in your sketchbook.

How to Make a Butterfly

You'll need to measure out enough yarn to complete your motif. The quantity table on page 36 will help you to calculate how much yarn you'll need for each chart. I'd recommend using no more than 15 - 20 metres/16 - 22yds for your butterfly to keep things manageable. As a rough estimate, when using felted tweed on 4mm needles (US 6), you'll average 50 stitches to one metre of yarn.

Lay one end of the yarn across your palm leaving an 8cm/3¼in tail that hangs below the bottom of your hand. It's this end of the yarn that you'll use to knit with.

Now take the other end of your yarn around the back of your thumb. Bring it to the front of your hand and then take it around the back of your middle or third finger before going around your thumb again in a figure of eight.

Keep winding the yarn around your finger and thumb in this figure of eight shape until you're left with approximately 10cm/4in of yarn.

Now wrap the 10cm/4in length around the back of your butterfly in the middle of the figure of eight. Catch the original tail as you bring the yarn up and over the front of your butterfly to continue wrapping around the center. Keep wrapping your 10cm/4in length around the middle of your butterfly until you almost reach the end.

Tuck the end through one of your wraps to secure and carefully slip the butterfly off your fingers.

The original tail left hanging is your working yarn.

Working In Color

I've always been very inspired by the colors around me. Color has played a significant role in my life and it's an endless source of creative inspiration. While there are tried and tested palettes, our perception of which colors work together is subjective and we're all drawn to different combinations. There are no rights and wrongs so it's important to approach color with confidence, rather than feeling inhibited by any lack of technical knowledge. As I often point out in my workshops, no one will have felt the need to choose their clothes with the help of a color wheel.

I think it's important to trust your instincts and to begin by working with the colors that you're naturally drawn to. You can then experiment with different palettes and have fun developing combinations that evoke your favorite memories.

I find it really helpful to create grids of complementary colors (using watercolors, colored pens or pencils), which I then arrange into seasonal palettes as part of my own color diary. Making grids like these will allow you to see how different colors work together until you find your favorite combinations. The grids themselves can even form the basis of a simple knitting project such as a cushion cover.

Playing around with your butterflies of yarn is also a great way of seeing how to build palettes and for developing your instinctive feel for color.

It's so rewarding to create a treasure box of favorite yarns and sketches and to see the colors come together as part of a stunning piece such as a quilt.

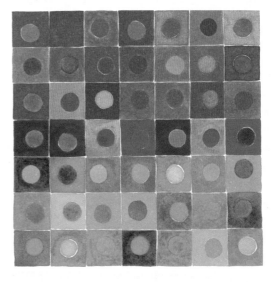

Example color grid with complementary colors.

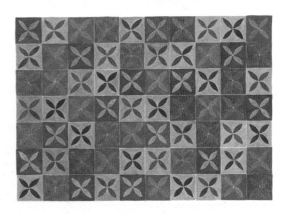

A simple flower petal design in my favorite berry colors.

How To Make Templates

Making a flower or leaf template

To make a flower or leaf template to form the basis of a chart, simply lay the flower or leaf directly onto a photocopier screen, carefully cover with a sheet of white paper, press the lid down and photocopy. I recommend photocopying onto good quality card that's not too thick for your photocopier since card cut-outs will last longer than paper. I use a sharp pair of scissors and a cutting knife and mat to cut out my template shapes and to keep the lines clearly defined. If you don't have access to a photocopier then simply trace around your leaf or flower to make the template and take a photograph for color reference.

To make a photocopy of an open flower head, cut the flower stem off close to the flower head without cutting into the flower. Lay the flower head face down on the photocopier screen and adjust the petals so they're not folded.

You can also press your flowers and leaves by laying them in between two sheets of parchment paper. Carefully place your covered flower in the center of a heavy book and lay other books on top to press everything down. It will take a good four weeks for your flowers and leaves to dry. When photocopying your dried flowers and leaves, be careful as they will now be very delicate.

Designing A Chart

Knitting is something I love to do with friends as much as I like knitting quietly on my own. My wonderful friend Georgie has been a great help and support in making this book and we've spent many happy days in the studio tangled in yarn!

There's a long and precious tradition of families and friends working together to make quilts, particularly for special occasions such as weddings and christenings, so why not invite people to join you and to get involved in every stage of the creative process?

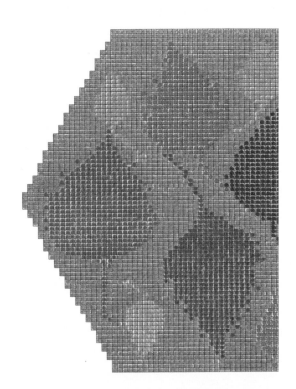

Designing your chart

Place the template(s) you've made onto a blank chart and experiment with the layout until you're happy with it. Trace around the shapes with a soft pencil (2B is perfect). Use X's to start marking where your stitches will go. Always start at the outer edges of your shapes since it's these outer stitches that are most important for the drawing element of your design. Don't make your X's too heavy as you want the freedom to erase easily until you have an outer edge of stitches that you're happy with.

When you're pleased with the stitches you've chosen for all the outside edges, use colored pencils or felt pens to color in your design. I use circles of color in each grid box. Refer to the charts in this book for guidance.

My Heirloom Quilt

My finished patchwork quilt is filled with special memories. You can, of course, choose to knit the same design but I hope you'll also feel inspired to create your very own heirloom quilt.

Knitting Pattern

Finished size: Full hexagon approx 30cm x 28cm/11¾ x 11¼in. My quilt is made up of 32 full hexagons, 6 upper/lower half-hexagons and 14 left/right hand half-hexagons. This gives a finished quilt of approximately 140cm x 200cm /55 x 78¾in. To make the body of my quilt, I knitted each of my 16 designs twice.

Yarn: #3 Light Weight Yarn (shown in Rowan Felted Tweed) Please refer to yarn quantities tables on page 36 for more information.

Needles: Pair of 4mm (US6) knitting needles

Gauge: 22 sts and 30 rows to 10cm/4in square measured over stockinette stitch using 4mm (US6) needles. *Note:* adjust needle size if necessary to obtain the correct gauge.

Notes: Beginning at row 1, your charts should be read from right to left for a right side (knit) row, and left to right for a wrong side (purl) row. Knit the first and last stitch of each row to give a visible seam allowance, and to help when joining your hexagon pieces.

Increase or decrease stitches as required 1 stitch in from the edge to ensure a smooth edge when joining your hexagon pieces.

To make a stitch on a knit row, use the point of your left hand needle to pick up the horizontal float (from the front) in between the stitch you have just knitted and the next stitch. Use your right hand needle to knit this new stitch through the back loop. On a purl row, pick up the float from the back and purl into the front of it. This will twist and tighten the stitch, preventing a hole from forming.

As a visual reference, I have highlighted the increase rows in green on the hexagon templates, and the decrease rows in red.

Full Hexagon - make 32

Using 4mm (US6) needles, cast on 36 sts. Using your color chart as a guide throughout, and beginning with a RS (K) row, work 82 rows of hexagon in stockinette stitch.
You should increase 1 st **at each end** of rows 4, 6, 8, 11, 13, 15, 17, 19, 21, 24, 26, 28, 30, 33, 36, 38 and 40 (70 sts)
RS increase row: K1, m1, k to last st, m1, k1.
WS increase row: K1, m1, p to last st, m1, k1.
You should decrease 1 st **at each end** of rows 44, 46, 48, 51, 54, 56, 58, 60, 63, 65, 67, 69, 71, 73, 76, 78 and 80 (36 sts)
RS decrease row: K1, k2togtbl, k to last 3 sts, k2tog, k1.
WS decrease row: K1, p2tog, p to last 3 sts, p2togtbl, k1.
Cast off knitwise.

Full Hexagon template:

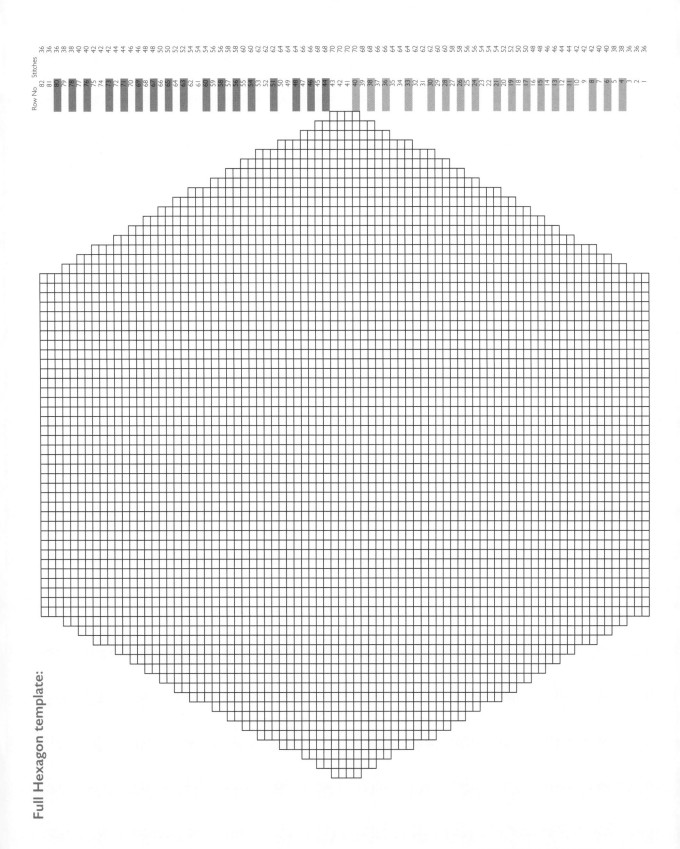

Upper / Lower Half-Hexagon (make 6)

Used as knitted for upper edge, and upside down for lower edge.

Using 4mm (US6) needles, cast on 36 sts.
Using the half-hexagon chart below as a guide, and beginning with a RS (K) row, work rows 1-42 of chart in stockinette stitch.
Increase 1 st **at each end** of rows 4, 6, 8, 11, 13, 15, 17, 19, 21, 24, 26, 28, 30, 33, 36, 38 and 40 (70 sts)
RS increase row: K1, m1, k to last st, m1, k1.
WS increase row: K1, m1, p to last st, m1, k1.
Cast off knitwise.

Abbreviations

K	Knit
K2tog	Knit 2 together
K2togtbl	Knit 2 together through back loop
M1	Make 1
P	Purl
P2tog	Purl 2 together
P2togtbl	Purl 2 together through back loop
RS	Right side
St/Sts	Stitch/Stiches
WS	Wrong side

Upper / Lower Half-Hexagon template:

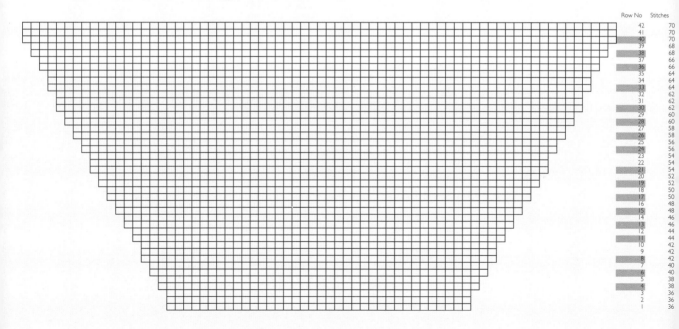

Row No	Stitches
42	70
41	70
40	70
39	68
38	68
37	66
36	66
35	64
34	64
33	64
32	62
31	62
30	62
29	60
28	60
27	58
26	58
25	56
24	56
23	54
22	54
21	54
20	52
19	52
18	50
17	50
16	48
15	48
14	46
13	46
12	44
11	44
10	42
9	42
8	42
7	40
6	40
5	38
4	38
3	36
2	36
1	36

Left / Right Hand edge (make 14)

Use as knitted for left hand edge, and upside down for right hand edge.

Please note for this side piece you will be increasing and decreasing on both right and wrong side rows, but always on the right hand edge of the hexagon as you look at the right side. So, for a right side row, shaping will be made at the beginning of the row, and for a wrong side row, shaping will be made at the end of the row.

Using 4mm (US6) needles, cast on 19 sts. Using the adjacent half-hexagon chart as a guide, and beginning with a RS (K) row, work all 82 rows of chart in stockinette stitch.

Increase 1 st **on the right hand edge of the right side ONLY** on rows 4, 6, 8, 11, 13, 15, 17, 19, 21, 24, 26, 28, 30, 33, 36, 38 and 40 (36 sts)

RS increase row: K1, m1, k to end.

WS increase row: K1, p to last st, m1, k1.

Decrease 1st **on the right hand side of the right side ONLY** on rows 44, 46, 48, 51, 54, 56, 58, 60, 63, 65, 67, 69, 71, 73, 76, 78, 80 (19 sts)

RS decrease row: K1, k2togtbl, k to end.

WS decrease row: K1, p to last 3 sts, p2togtbl, k1.

Cast off knitwise.

Left / Right edge template:

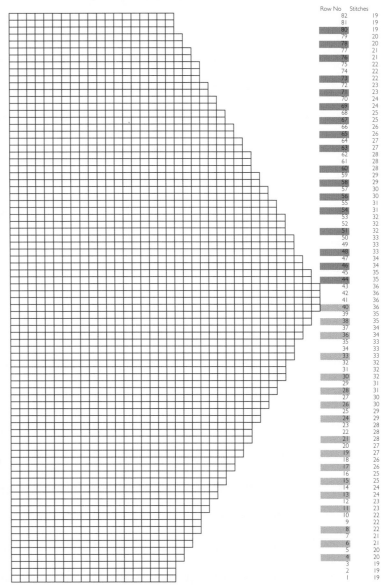

Row No	Stitches
82	19
81	19
80	19
79	20
78	20
77	21
76	21
75	22
74	22
73	22
72	23
71	23
70	24
69	24
68	25
67	25
66	26
65	26
64	27
63	27
62	28
61	28
60	28
59	29
58	29
57	30
56	30
55	31
54	31
53	32
52	32
51	32
50	33
49	33
48	33
47	34
46	34
45	35
44	35
43	36
42	36
41	36
40	36
39	35
38	35
37	34
36	34
35	33
34	33
33	33
32	32
31	32
30	32
29	31
28	31
27	30
26	30
25	29
24	29
23	28
22	28
21	28
20	27
19	27
18	26
17	26
16	25
15	25
14	24
13	24
12	23
11	23
10	22
9	22
8	22
7	21
6	21
5	20
4	20
3	19
2	19
1	19

Hexagon Templates to copy for creating your own designs:

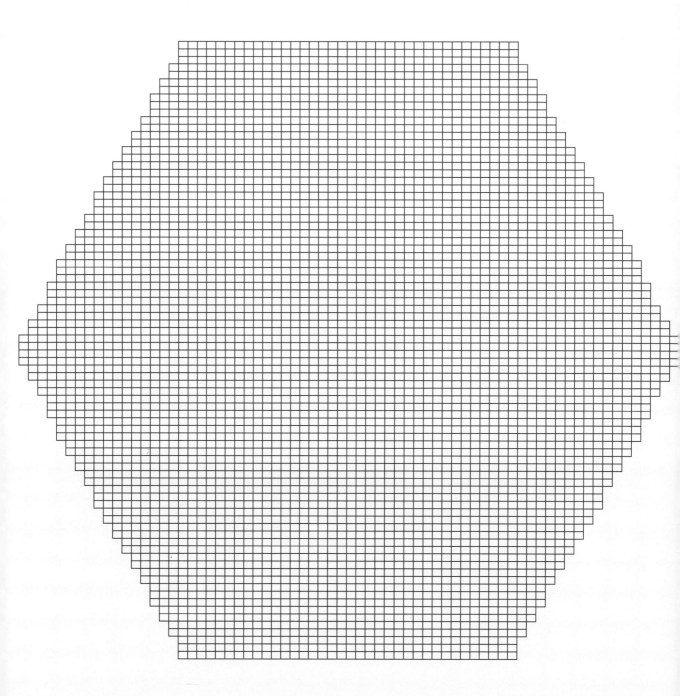

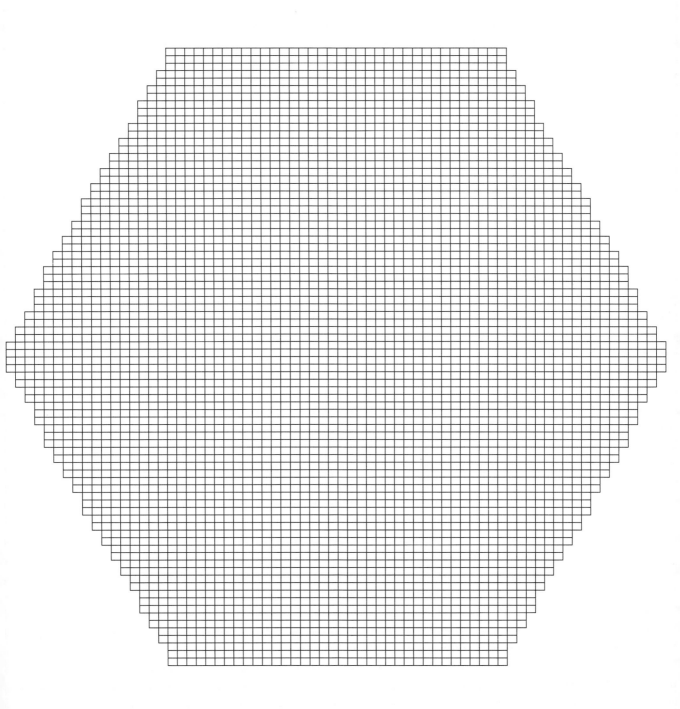

Yarn Quantities

This table gives a guide to the amount of yarn used to knit up one of each of my hexagon designs.

To make my quilt, I knitted each of these designs twice.

The second table, showing the number of balls of each yarn required to knit my quilt, allows for the fact that each hexagon has been knitted twice.

Hexagon	Rowan Felted Tweed (#3 Light Weight Yarn)														
	Treacle (dark brown) 145	Rage (deep red) 150	Bilberry (purple) 151	Maritime (pale blue) 167	Ginger (dark orange) 154	Pine (dark green) 158	Avocado (bright green) 161	Watery (aqua blue) 152	Clay (light gray) 177	Seasalter (blue) 178	Mineral (yellow) 181	Peony (deep pink) 183	Frozen (light pink) 185	Tawny (maroon) 186	Amethyst (light purple) 192
Anemones		26m/29yds	15m/17yds				40m/44yds	20m/22yds	6m/7yds	6m/7yds					
Tulips						4m/5yds	26m/29yds					8m/9yds	52m/57yds		
Crocus				26m/29yds	2m/3yds							65m/71yds			
Tulips & Muscari					18m/20yds		18m/20yds	45m/50yds		10m/11yds	10m/11yds				
Sunflower	10m/11yds				17m/19yds			60m/66yds			34m/38yds				
Pressed Roses		15m/17yds				62m/68yds	8m/9yds					10m/11yds			
Peony										45m/50yds		20m/22yds	20m/22yds	20m/22yds	
Hydrangea						10m/11yds	35m/39yds				3m/3yds	30m/33yds			25m/28yds
Autumn Leaves	7m/8yds	10m/11yds		55m/61yds	9m/10yds	8m/9yds					6m/7yds				
Autumn Stripes	15m/17yds	15m/17yds		30m/33yds	25m/28yds		15m/17yds								
Maple Leaf		65m/71yds					30m/33yds								
Myrtle & Roses		7m/8yds	5m/6yds	15m/17yds	75m/82yds		10m/11yds	20m/22yds		5m/6yds		2m/3yds			
Holly		10m/11yds	75m/82yds				25m/28yds				10m/11yds				
Snowdrops							5m/6yds		6m/7yds	72m/79yds					
Violets			29m/32yds					93m/102yds			3m/3yds				
Winter Berries			8m/9yds	10m/11yds			6m/7yds	5m/6yds			60m/66yds			8m/9yds	

The upper/lower edge pieces and left/right hand edge pieces use approximately 40m/44yds of Rowan Felted Tweed each.

If knitting my quilt, you should have enough yarn left to knit the 20 edge pieces in a variety of colors with the yarn quantities outlined here.

If using Rowan Felted Tweed;

Yarn	Color	Code	Ball Length	Balls Required
Rowan Felted Tweed	Treacle	145	175m	1
Rowan Felted Tweed	Rage	150	175m	3
Rowan Felted Tweed	Bilberry	151	175m	2
Rowan Felted Tweed	Maritime	167	175m	3
Rowan Felted Tweed	Ginger	154	175m	2
Rowan Felted Tweed	Pine	158	175m	1
Rowan Felted Tweed	Avocado	161	175m	3
Rowan Felted Tweed	Watery	152	175m	2
Rowan Felted Tweed	Clay	177	175m	1
Rowan Felted Tweed	Seasalter	178	175m	2
Rowan Felted Tweed	Mineral	181	175m	3
Rowan Felted Tweed	Peony	183	175m	2
Rowan Felted Tweed	Frozen	185	175m	1
Rowan Felted Tweed	Tawny	186	175m	1
Rowan Felted Tweed	Amethyst	192	175m	1

Finishing Your Quilt

When you've completed your knitted hexagons, weave in all ends and block or lightly press each hexagon. You will use the single stitch at each end of each row as your seam allowance. Sew your ends back into the hexagon. This keeps loose ends free from your seam allowance when sewing pieces together. Don't worry if your hexagons look slightly uneven as everything will come together when you join the pieces using mattress stitch. You may wish to block again when all of the pieces have been stitched together.

Before sewing your quilt together, look at the image on page 27 as a guide to laying out your pieces. When you're happy with the arrangement, you can sew the quilt together. I used mattress stitch, and began by joining the cast off edge of one hexagon to the cast on edge of the next until I had all my vertical strips. Then, I sewed the vertical seams of my strips together with mattress stitch. Match your sewing yarn to the base color of one of the 2 hexagons you're stitching together at any one time so that your seam is as invisible as possible.

Mattress Stitch

Mattress stitch is a lovely way to join two pieces of knitting together since it creates a neat, flat, invisible seam. If you've never worked mattress stitch before, practice joining a couple of 10cm/4in gauge squares together so that you're comfortable with the technique before you start sewing your quilt together.

How to make a vertical seam when joining two stockinette stitch pieces together:

When joining your hexagon pieces together, work with the right side facing you. To sew your two pieces together, use the horizontal bars in between your stitches and work the seam from the bottom of your two pieces to the top. Work the seam one stitch in from the edge of your knitted pieces.

To begin, run your needle under the first stitch on the bottom left piece then bring the needle across and run it under the first stitch on the bottom of the piece you're joining.

Take your needle across to the left piece and run the needle under the first horizontal bar in between the first and second stitch. Take your needle across to the other piece you're joining and do the same on the corresponding bar, running your needle under the bar in between the first two stitches. You don't need to work underneath every bar in between the stitches; every two, three or four bars is fine.

Alternate from one side to the other, working each corresponding bar until you've sewn up to the top of your seam.

Give the yarn a little tug to bring the two sides together. Run your needle under the last stitch on the left hand side and across and under the last stitch on the right hand side. Pull together and sew in loose ends on the wrong side.

The process is exactly the same to join a cast on / cast off edge except that you use the holes between the V's of worked stitches.

To complete my quilt, I worked 2 rounds of double crochet (US single crochet) with a 3.75mm (US F/5) crochet hook around the edge once I had sewn all my pieces together. This gave me a lovely neat, flat edge. You could use any leftover yarn to make a deeper border.

My Heirloom Quilt Charts

My finished patchwork quilt is filled with special memories. You can, of course, choose to knit the same design but I hope you'll also feel inspired to create your very own heirloom quilt.

Spring for me is the awakening of all the seasons and a blossoming
of the year ahead.

Anemones

Anemones are one of my favorite spring flowers and
probably the flower I treat myself to the most in spring.
When the house is full of their happy, bright colors
I know that spring is here and I'm soon laying out
the watercolors!

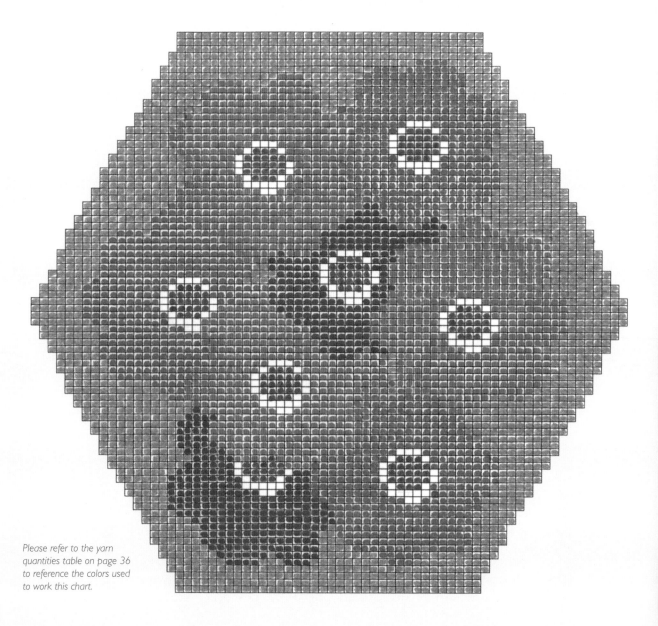

*Please refer to the yarn
quantities table on page 36
to reference the colors used
to work this chart.*

Tulips

Tulips are fabulous flowers. They're easy to grow and so much fun to watch as their big, bold leaves unfold. The large yellow tulips that inspired this chart are yearly visitors in my little and invitingly overgrown garden.

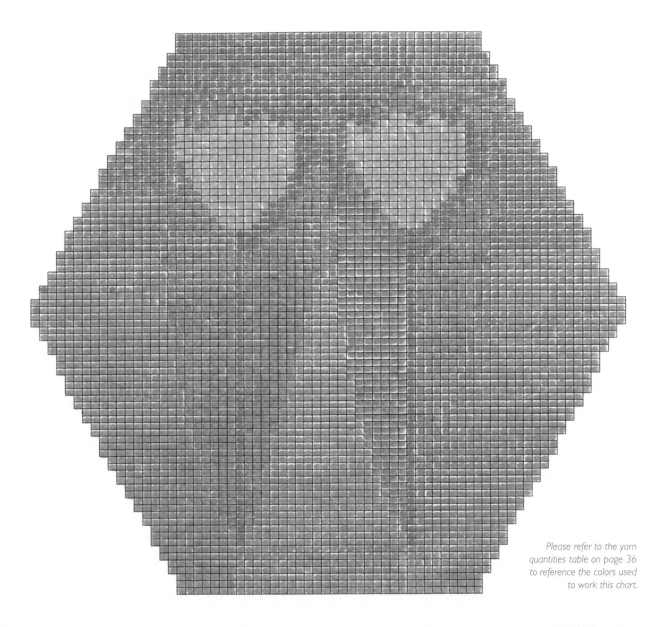

Please refer to the yarn quantities table on page 36 to reference the colors used to work this chart.

Crocuses

Crocuses emerge from the soil in spring, creating
a carpet of beautiful blues and purples – a striking
contrast to the pale yellow sunlight on a warm spring
day – and form a colorful palette in my
spring garden.

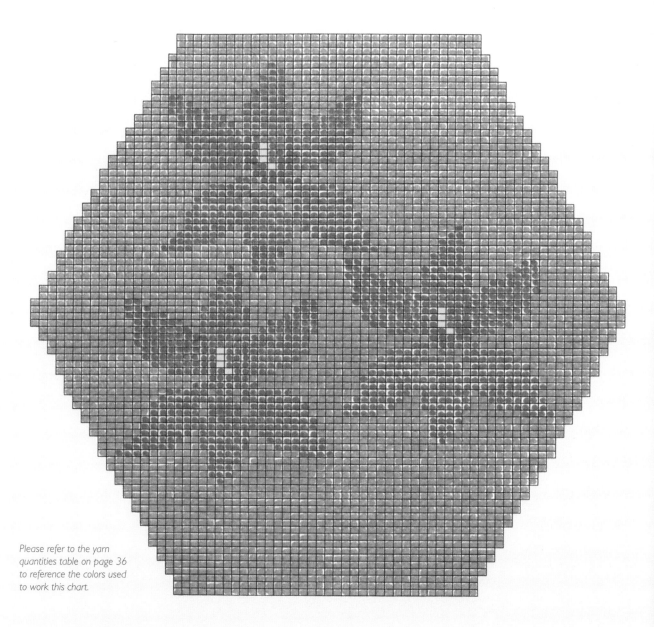

*Please refer to the yarn
quantities table on page 36
to reference the colors used
to work this chart.*

Tulips & Muscari

Tulips and muscari are a favorite combination for christening arrangements. My very talented friend and florist, Emma, uses this wonderful combination of flowers for many of her christening commissions. It's always so inspiring to walk into Emma's shop on a spring morning and to see the colorful bouquets coming together.

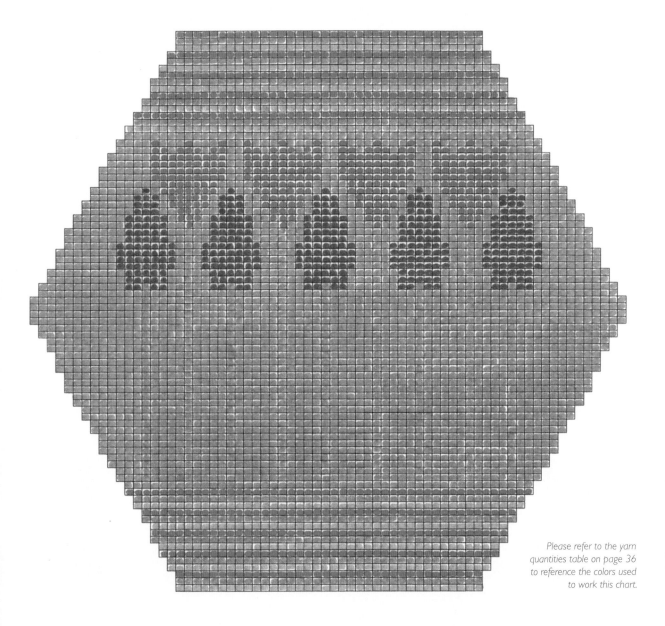

Please refer to the yarn quantities table on page 36 to reference the colors used to work this chart.

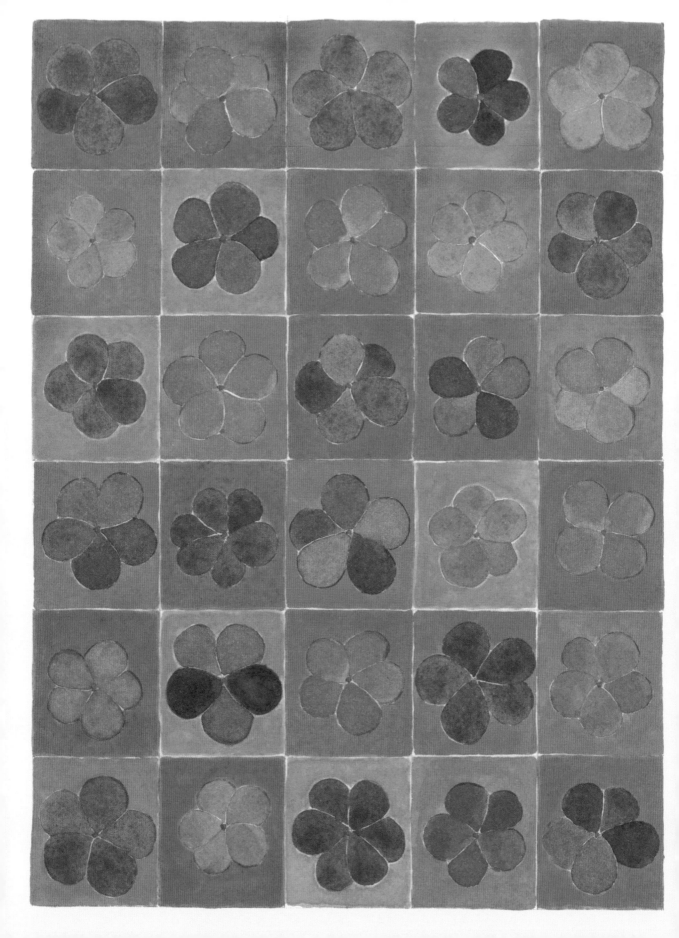

Summer brings warmth, celebrations and the joy of holidays filled
with carefree afternoons.

Sunflower

When my son Noah was young we planted sunflower
seeds and grew great big yellow sunflowers in our
garden every summer. Even when the petals had fallen
off, we had fun collecting the seeds from the beautiful
cream, black-brown center.

*Please refer to the yarn
quantities table on page 36
to reference the colors used
to work this chart.*

Pressed Roses

My birthday is in late August and during one birthday visit to Bath my husband bought me a bouquet full of blush pink and fuchsia-colored roses. It was a perfect late summer's day spent with my family. When I got home I pressed a couple of the buds and dried the rest of the bouquet. I still have the dried bouquet. It sits on a shelf in my kitchen and I smile every time it catches my eye.

Please refer to the yarn quantities table on page 36 to reference the colors used to work this chart.

Peony

When we moved into our house some years ago, we inherited a small garden with many established plants. My peony sits just outside the kitchen door and is my favorite. It's a deep pink and very romantic, and I cut stems when the heads grow large and heavy. Their delicately sweet smell fills my kitchen with the familiar scent of summer. Although peonies don't flower for long, as soon as I see their burgundy shoots pushing through the soil, I feel the excitement of warm summer days to come.

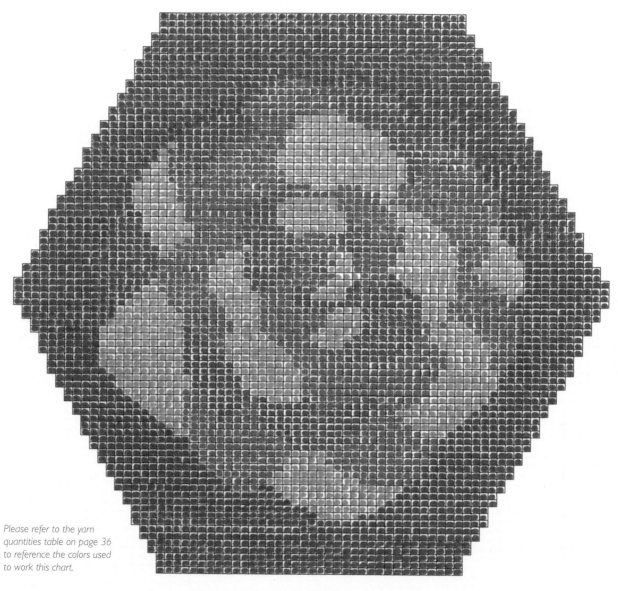

Please refer to the yarn quantities table on page 36 to reference the colors used to work this chart.

Hydrangeas

A ready-made bouquet in palettes of dusky pinks and purples, saturated blues and faded whites, these flowers bring a burst of color, pattern and volume to a summer garden. I have a large hydrangea that sits next to my front door and during the summer and well into the autumn, I'm greeted with clusters of pretty pastel pinks. I press the petals and they inspire many of my patterns and paintings.

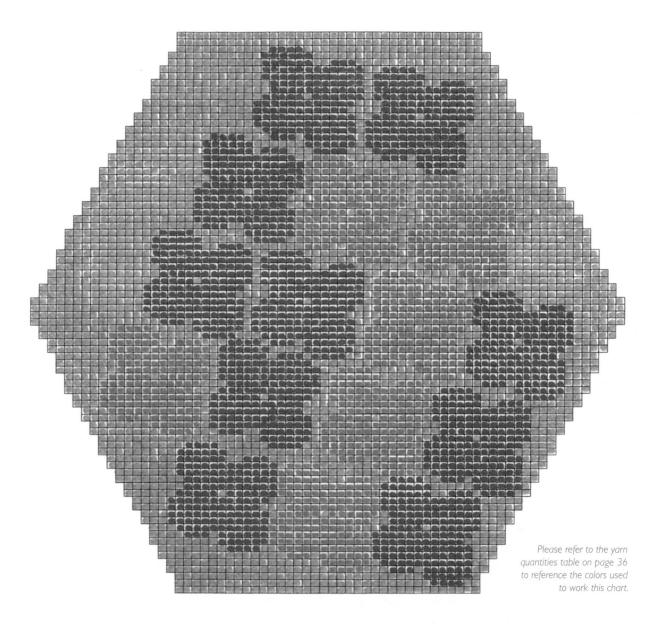

Please refer to the yarn quantities table on page 36 to reference the colors used to work this chart.

Autumn brings a rich palette of color and texture. The fresh chill in the air gives me a burst of creative energy.

Autumn Leaves

When I think of all the seasons, it's autumn colors that I'm drawn to the most. I collect leaves every autumn and I never fail to find new shapes and color combinations. I always look forward to the inspiration and excitement that the autumn palette brings.

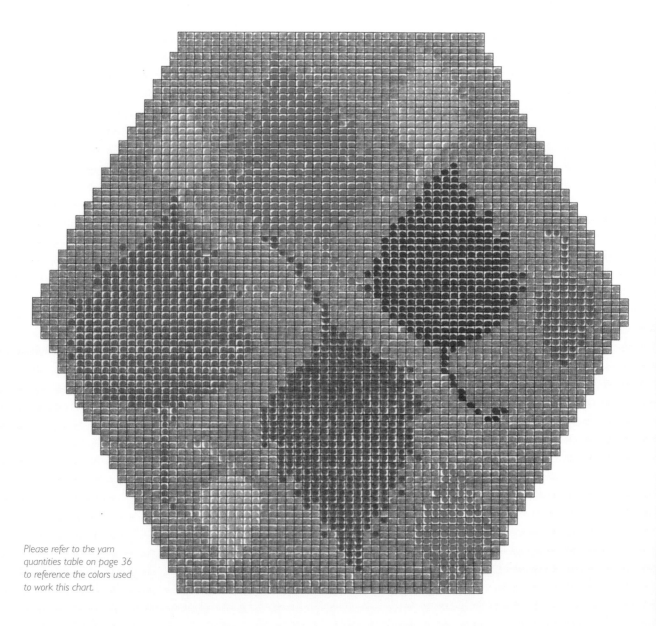

Please refer to the yarn quantities table on page 36 to reference the colors used to work this chart.

Autumn Stripes

Stripes and other geometric shapes are popular motifs in knitting. Most of my color palettes are drawn from nature, and the striped pattern on this chart was inspired by a leaf I found in front of my house one crisp autumn morning. The dominant colors were orange and blue-green, with a large patch of red and small areas of brown. I've reflected the proportion of the colors on the leaf in the depth of each row on this chart.

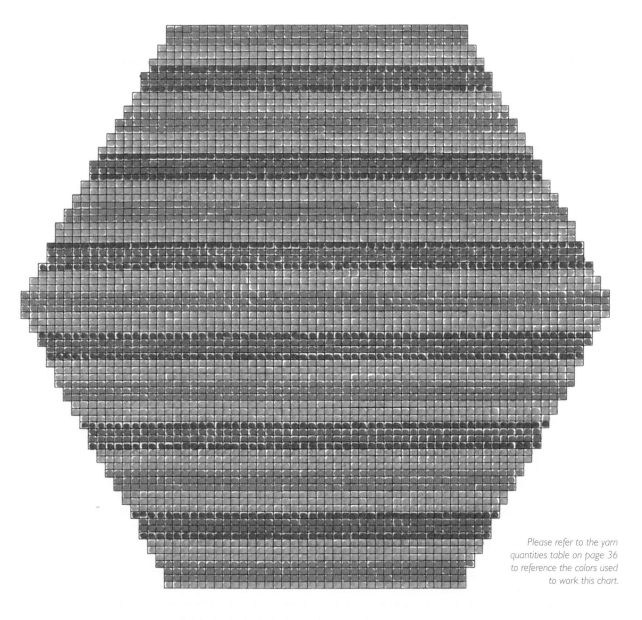

Please refer to the yarn quantities table on page 36 to reference the colors used to work this chart.

Maple Leaf

A maple leaf is a perfect shape for the intarsia technique. It's a great shape to start with when designing your own charts since it's interesting to work with and not too difficult to chart.

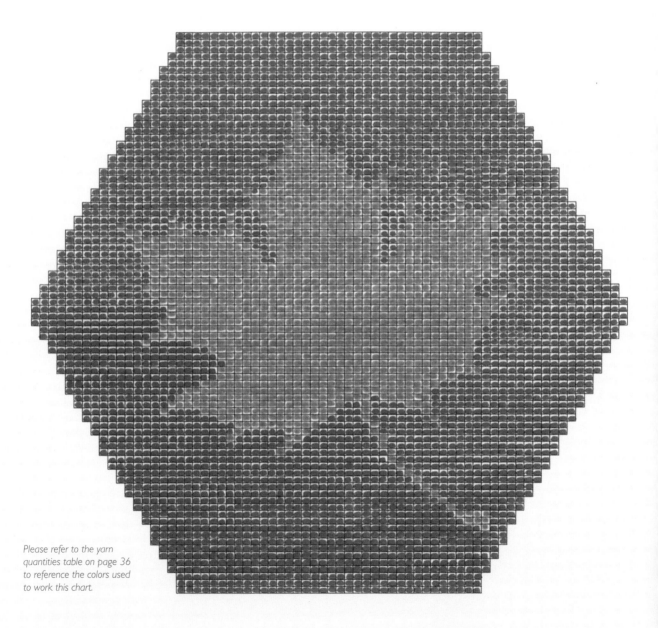

Please refer to the yarn quantities table on page 36 to reference the colors used to work this chart.

Myrtle & Roses

Sometimes it isn't a flower-filled occasion or time in the garden that inspires me but a trip to a beautiful florist. I'm lucky to have one near me and I often treat myself to flowers from the gorgeous selection of the day when I'm popping into my local market town. Saturday mornings also include a visit to my local wool shop and I often take my flowers in so that I can choose yarns to match them and create an inspiring palette. Myrtle and roses are a favorite autumn combination which features in many of my watercolors and designs.

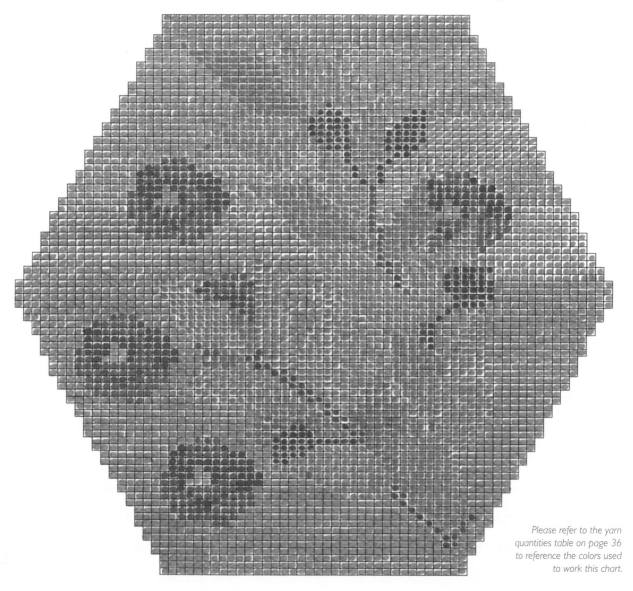

Please refer to the yarn quantities table on page 36 to reference the colors used to work this chart.

Winter is a time of festive celebrations, seeing friends, baking and bold, jewel-like colors.

Holly

Holly, berries and rich, regal colors are so evocative of the Christmas season and feature abundantly in my festive designs.

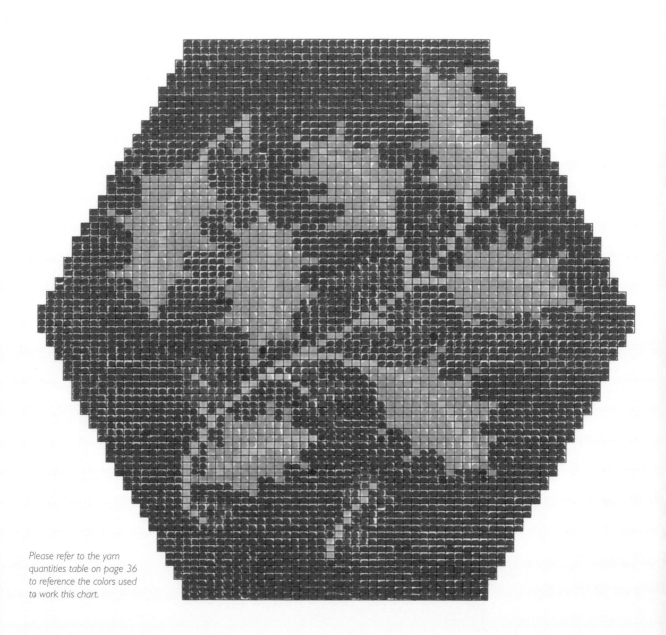

Please refer to the yarn quantities table on page 36 to reference the colors used to work this chart.

Snowdrops

Although snowdrops are a spring bulb, they always appear in my garden in late winter.
Delicately layered white flowers nod over thin mint-green stems. Emerging through the earth
under steely gray skies, snowdrops bring the promise of warmer days to come.

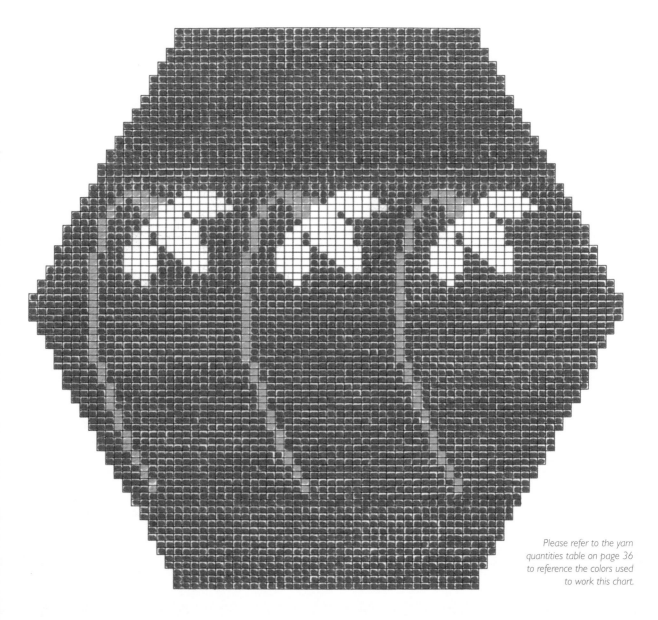

*Please refer to the yarn
quantities table on page 36
to reference the colors used
to work this chart.*

SNOWDROPS **67**

Violets

Richard and I were married in the month of December in a simple, beautiful ceremony. My bouquet was made from closely gathered violets, hand-tied with an ivory silk ribbon. The richness of the deep violet color worked in perfect harmony with my silk-satin ivory dress and the bright blue winter sky.

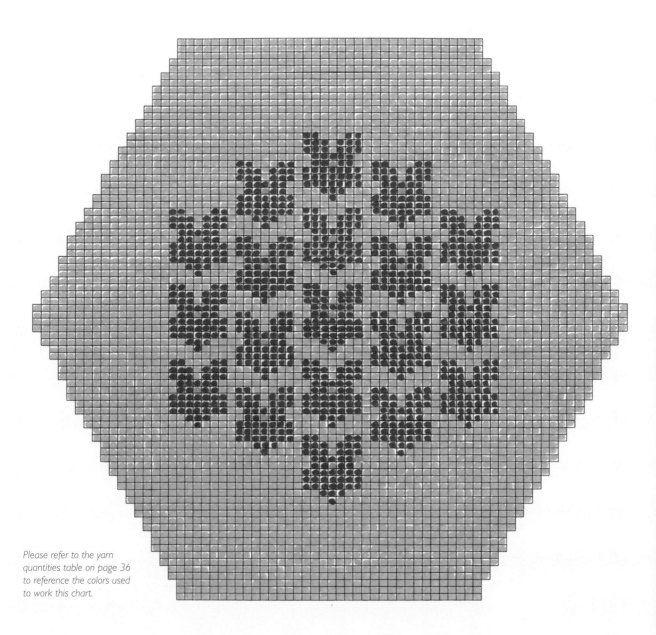

Please refer to the yarn quantities table on page 36 to reference the colors used to work this chart.

Winter Berries

The country lanes around my home are lined with hedgerows that burst with vibrant red, blue-black and rich purple berries in the winter. These little jewels of color inspire bold winter palettes and accent colors.

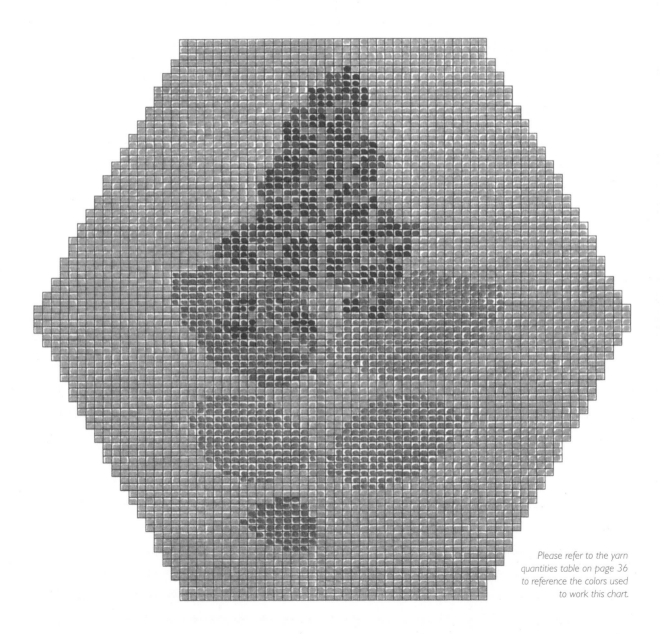

Please refer to the yarn quantities table on page 36 to reference the colors used to work this chart.

Further Projects

Purse

Finished size: Approx 12cm x 12cm / 4¾ x 4¾in

Yarn: Approx 32m/35yds x #3 Light Weight Yarn (shown in Rowan Felted Tweed Watery 152) for your background color, plus small pieces of yarn as required for intarsia and embroidery detail

Needles: Pair of 3.25mm (US3) knitting needles

Extras:
65mm/2½in sew-in purse frame
Darning needle

Gauge: 26sts and 36 rows to 10cm/4in square measured over stockinette stitch using 3.25mm (US 3) needles or needles required to obtain correct gauge.

Notes: Beginning at row 1, your chart should be read from right to left for a right side (knit) row and from left to right for a wrong side (purl) row.

The base of the purse body is worked in short rows. To avoid holes forming, you are required to wrap a stitch at the end of each short row.

For a knit row, pass the yarn between your needles to the front of your work.

Slip the next stitch onto your right hand needle, and take the yarn back between your needles.

Slip the stitch back to your left hand needle. For a purl row, take the yarn between your needles to the back of your work.

Slip the next stitch onto your right hand needle, and bring the yarn back between your needles.

Slip the stitch back to your left hand needle. In both cases the wrapped stitch remains unworked, but has a wrap around the base of it.

Purse Body (make 2):
Using 3.25mm (US3) needles and background color yarn, cast on 31 sts.
Working from chart, continue in stockinette stitch, incorporating the intarsia motif where required as follows:

Row 1: K18, wrap next st and turn.
Row 2: P5, wrap next st and turn.
Row 3: K7, wrap next st and turn.
Row 4: P9, wrap next st and turn.
Continue as set, working 2 extra sts at the end of each short row until you have completed row 14. Both end sts now have a wrap on them.
Row 15: K30.
Row 16: P31. (31 sts)
You have now incorporated all 31 sts into your work.
Rows 17-24: Work 8 rows in stockinette stitch, continuing to incorporate the intarsia motif as required.
Row 25: K1, k2togtbl, k to last 3 sts, k2tog, k1. (29 sts)

Row 26: K1, p to last st, k1.
Repeat last 2 rows twice more .(25 sts)

Purse Frame shaping
Cast off 3 sts at beginning of next 2 rows.
(19 sts)
Row 33: K1, k2togtbl, k to last 3 sts, k2tog, k1.
(17 sts)
Row 34: K1, p to last st, k1.
Repeat last 2 rows four times more. (9 sts)
Row 43: K1, k2togtbl, k3, k2tog, k1. (7 sts)
Row 44: K1, p2tog, p1, p2togtbl, k1. (5 sts)
Cast off.

Making Up
Block or press the purse bodies to size, and
weave in ends. Embroider detail onto your
design using split stitch as desired. With right
sides together, sew purse bodies together below
purse frame shaping. Turn right side out. Working
each side of purse body separately, fit and stitch
purse bodies into purse frame.

To Work Split Stitch
Using yarn double, make a small stitch, approx
3-5mm in your work. To make the next stitch,
bring the needle up halfway through this stitch,
splitting the yarn as you do. Make this stitch
the same length as the last, and again bring the
needle up through this stitch, splitting the yarn as
you work, to begin forming the next stitch.

Try not to pull your stitches too tightly or you
will lose them in the knit stitches.

The aim is that the embroidery sits on top of
the knitted stitches.

Leaf Motif Chart

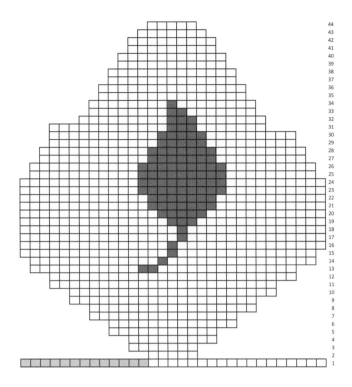

Blank Chart

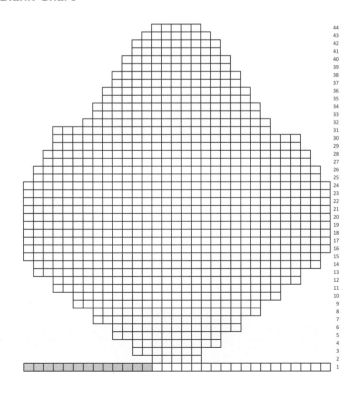

Bunting

Yarn: Approx 25m/28yds x #3 Light Weight Yarn (shown in Rowan Felted Tweed) in background color plus short lengths as required for intarsia detail. and crochet chain

Needles: Pair of 4mm (US6) knitting needles & 4mm (USG/6) crochet hook.

Gauge: 22 sts and 30 rows to 10cm (4in) square measured over stockinette stitch using 4mm (US6) needles or needles required to obtain correct gauge.

Bunting Flag

Throughout this pattern you "make" stitches to give the triangular shape. To keep a neat edge, make the stitch one stitch in from the edge of your work. To "make" a stitch on a knit row, use the point of your left hand needle to pick up the horizontal float (from the front) in between the stitch you have just knitted and the next stitch. Use your right hand needle to knit this new stitch through the back loop. This will twist and tighten the stitch, preventing a hole from forming. It is also good practice to knit the first and last stitches of each wrong side row to give you a nice flat edge.

Using 4mm (US6) needles, make a slip knot, and slide it onto your needle.

Foundation Rows

Row 1 (RS): Knit. (1 st)
Row 2 (WS): Knit into the front and back of the stitch. (2 sts)
Row 3: K1, m1, k1. (3 sts)

Working from chart, continue as follows:
Row 4: K1, p1, k1.
Row 5: K1, m1, k1, m1, k1. (5 sts)
Row 6: K1, p3, k1.
Row 7: K1, m1, k3, m1, k1. (7 sts)
Row 8: K1, p5, k1.
Continue as set, increasing 1 st at each end of every right side row and incorporating the intarsia motif required until you have 45 sts, ending with a right side row.
Next row (WS): K1, purl to last st, k1.
Knit 4 rows.
Cast off knitwise.

Making Up

Work a chain of 50 double crochet (US single crochet) then pick up along the top edge of your first bunting triangle, then space the remaining triangles evenly every 25 chain stitches along the length. Finish with a chain of 50 stitches.

For the Muscari head, detail by using French Knots.

Tulip Motif

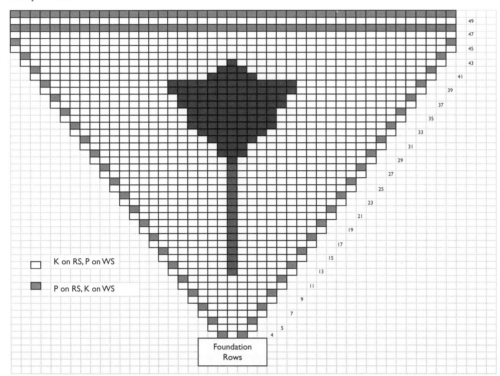

K on RS, P on WS

P on RS, K on WS

49
47
45
43
41
39
37
35
33
31
29
27
25
23
21
19
17
15
13
11
9
7
5
4

Foundation Rows

Rose Motif

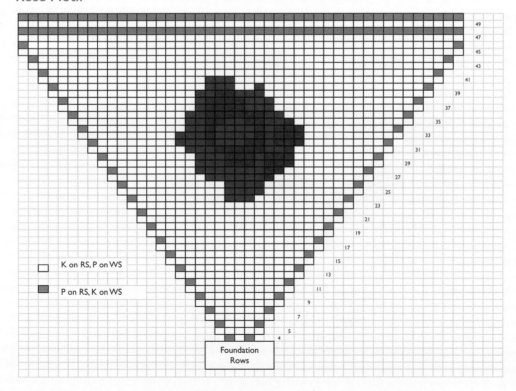

K on RS, P on WS

P on RS, K on WS

49
47
45
43
41
39
37
35
33
31
29
27
25
23
21
19
17
15
13
11
9
7
5
4

Foundation Rows

Muscari Motif

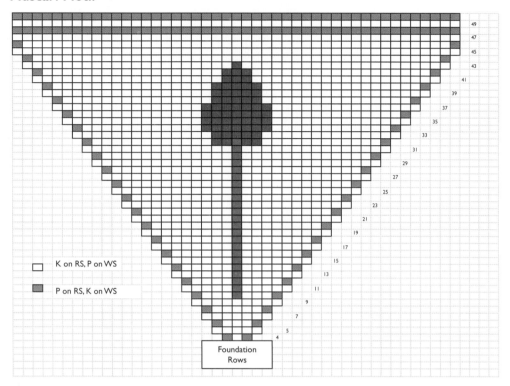

K on RS, P on WS

P on RS, K on WS

Foundation
Rows

4 5 7 9 11 13 15 17 19 21 23 25 27 29 31 33 35 37 39 41 43 45 47 49

Butterfly Motif

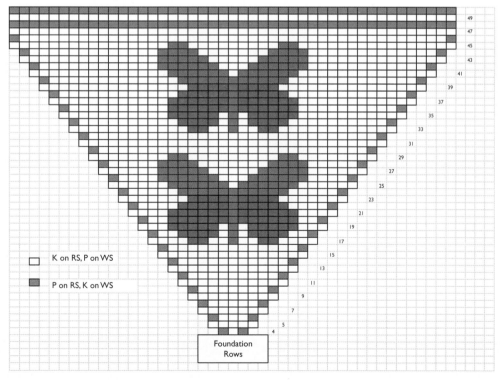

K on RS, P on WS

P on RS, K on WS

Foundation
Rows

4 5 7 9 11 13 15 17 19 21 23 25 27 29 31 33 35 37 39 41 43 45 47 49

Buttons

Finished size: Approx 4cm x 4cm /1½ x 1½in to fit a 29mm/1¼in self-cover button.

Yarn: Approx 4m/5yds x #3 Light Weight Yarn (shown in Rowan Felted Tweed) in background color plus short lengths as required for intarsia detail and embroidery.

Needles: Pair of 3.25mm (US3) knitting needles

Extras:
29mm/1¼in self-cover buttons
Darning needle

Gauge: 32 sts and 36 rows to 10cm/4in square measured over stockinette stitch using 3.25 mm (US3) needles or needles required to obtain correct gauge.

Notes: Beginning at row 1, the charts should be read from right to left for a right side (knit) row and from left to right for a wrong side (purl) row.

Button Cover
Using 3.25mm (US 3) needles and background color yarn, cast on 13 sts.

Beginning with a knit row, work in stockinette stitch for 14 rows, incorporating intarsia motif where required.
Cast off knitwise.

Making Up
Block or press your button cover to size as preferred, and sew in ends.

Embroider detail as desired. Stretch over the top of your self-cover button, and snap secure as instructed according to your specific button.

To Work Split Stitch
Make a small stitch of approx 3-5mm in your work using a double strand of #2 Fine Yarn (shown in Rowan Fine Lace).

To make the next stitch, bring the needle up halfway through this stitch, splitting the yarn as you do. Make this stitch the same length as the last, and again bring the needle up through this stitch, splitting the yarn as you work, to begin forming the next stitch.

Try not to pull your stitches too tightly or you will lose them in the knit stitches.

The aim is that the embroidery sits on top of the knitted stitches.

Charts

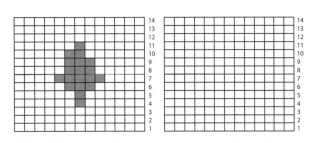

Rose Brooch

Finished size: Approx 10cm x 8cm/4 x 3¼in

Yarn: Short lengths of soft pink #2 Fine Yarn (shown in Rowan Fine Lace, Charity 941), dark purple #3 Light Weight Yarn (shown in Rowan Felted Tweed, Bilberry 151), deep red #3 Light Weight Yarn (shown in Rowan Felted Tweed, Tawny 186) and soft pink #3 Light Weight Yarn (shown in Rowan Felted Tweed, Frozen 185)

Needles: Pair of 3.25mm (US3) knitting needles

Extras:
Brooch pin
Darning needle

Gauge: 28 sts and 36 rows to 10cm/4in square measured over stockinette stitch using 3.25 mm (US3) needles or needles required to obtain correct gauge.

Notes:
You will "make" stitches to shape your heart. Make each stitch one stitch in from the edge of your work, and knit the first and last stitches of each wrong side row. To make a stitch on a knit row, use the point of your left hand needle to pick up the horizontal float (from the front) in between the stitch you have just knitted and the next stitch. Use your right hand needle to knit this new stitch through the back loop. On a purl row, pick up the float from the back and purl into the front of it. This will twist and tighten the stitch, preventing a hole from forming.

Large Heart

Using deep red #3 Light Weight Yarn (shown in Rowan Felted Tweed, Tawny 186), make a slip knot and slide it on to your needle.

Work foundation rows as follows:
Row 1 (RS): Knit. (1 st)
Row 2 (WS): Knit into the front and back of the stitch. (2 sts)
Working from chart, continue in stockinette stitch as follows:
Row 3 (RS): K1, m1, k1. (3 sts)
Continue as set, incorporating the intarsia motif where required and increasing 1 stitch at each end of rows 4, 5, 6, 7, 8, 10, 11, 13, 14, 16, 18, 20 and 22, ending with a WS row. (29 sts)
Rows 23-28: Work in stockinette stitch for 6 rows, ending with right side (RS) facing for next row.
Row 29: K1, k2togtbl, k11 and turn, leaving remaining sts unworked.
Row 30: K1, p2tog, p7, p2togtbl, k1. (11 sts)
Row 31: K1, k2togtbl, k5, k2tog, k1. (9 sts)
Row 32: K1, p2tog, p3, p2togtbl, k1. (7 sts)
Row 33: K1, k2togtbl, k1, k2tog, k1. (5 sts)
Cast off these 5 sts.
With right side facing, rejoin yarn to remaining 15 sts.
Next Row (RS): Cast off 1 st, k to last 3 sts, k2tog, k1. (13 sts)
Repeat from row 30 to complete second side of heart shaping.

Small Heart

Using soft pink #3 Light Weight Yarn (shown in Rowan Felted Tweed, Frozen 185), make a slip knot and slide it on to your needle.

Work foundation rows as given for large heart. Working from chart, continue in stockinette stitch as follows:

Row 3 (RS): K1, m1, k1. (3 sts)

Continue as set, incorporating the intarsia motif where required and increasing 1 stitch at each end of rows 4, 5, 6, 7, 9, 11, 12, 14, 16 and 18, ending with a wrong side row. (23 sts).

Rows 19-21: Work in stockinette stitch for 3 rows.

Row 22: K1, p9, k1 and turn.

Row 23: K1, k2togtbl, k to end. (10 sts)

Row 24: K1, p2tog, p4, p2togtbl, k1. (8 sts)

Row 25: K1, k2togtbl, k2, k2tog, k1. (6 sts)

Row 26: K1, p2tog, p2togtbl, k1. (4 sts)

Cast off these 4 sts.

With wrong side facing, rejoin yarn to remaining 12 sts.

Next row (WS): Cast off 1 st, p to last st, k1. (11 sts)

Next Row: K8, k2togtbl, k1. (10 sts)

Repeat from row 24 to complete second side.

Making Up

Block or press each heart as preferred, and weave in ends. Using image as a guide, define the rose motif on your small heart using split stitch and a double strand of soft pink #2 Fine Yarn (shown in Rowan Fine Lace, Charity 941), with a dark purple #3 Light Weight Yarn (shown in Rowan Felted Tweed, Bilberry 151), French knot in the center. Stitch the small heart on top of the large heart using split stitch in dark purple #2 Fine Yarn (shown in Rowan Fine Lace, Era 927). Secure brooch pin to back of large heart.

To Make A French Knot

Bring a length of yarn approximately 30cm/11¾in up through the work where you want to position the French knot, leaving a tail of approximately 15cm/6in behind your work.

With the point of your needle held flat close to where the yarn is coming through your work, wrap the yarn towards you and around the needle 2-3 times, depending on the size of knot desired. Using your free hand to keep the yarn fairly taught, and keeping the wraps on your needle, push the point of your needle back through your work to the wrong side, very close to the point you brought it up.

Slowly draw the yarn through to the wrong side, using your free hand to help the wraps form a little knot as you do.

Gently pull both ends of your thread on the wrong side to hold your knot against the surface of your work on the right side, and secure.

To Work Split Stitch

Make a small stitch of approx 3-5mm in your work using a double strand of #2 Fine Yarn (shown in Rowan Fine Lace). To make the next stitch, bring the needle up halfway through this stitch, splitting the yarn as you do. Make this stitch the same length as the last, and again bring the needle up through this stitch, splitting the yarn as you work, to begin forming the next stitch. Try not to pull your stitches too tightly or you will lose them in the knit stitches.

The aim is that the embroidery sits on top of the knitted stitches.

Large Heart Chart

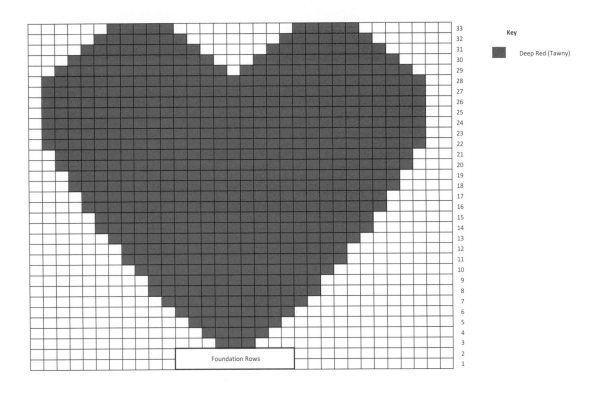

Small Heart Chart

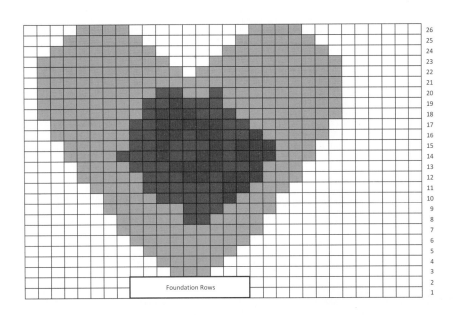

Project Bag

Finished size: Approx 25cm × 12.5cm × 18cm (9¾ × 5 × 7in) plus handles.

Yarn: 175m/192yds × #3 Light Weight Yarn (shown in Rowan Felted Tweed) for your background color, plus short lengths as required for intarsia detail. When starting out designing, I would suggest using a neutral color (for example Rowan Felted Tweed, Clay 177) as your background color as it is a good canvas that works well with any other color on top.

Needles: Pair of 4mm (US6) knitting needles

Extras:
Bag handles (125mm/5in diameter wooden hoops)
Cardboard for bag inner
Lining fabric of your choice
Darning needle
Fabric adhesive
Pins
Scissors
Hole punch
Sewing needle

Gauge: 22 sts and 30 rows to 10cm/4in square measured over stockinette stitch using 4mm (US6) needles or needles required to obtain correct gauge.

Bag Body
Using 4mm (US 6) needles and background color, cast on 170 sts.
Row 1 (RS): Knit 1, *knit across 28 sts of row 1 of chart, repeat from * 5 times more, k1.

Row 2 (WS): Knit 1, *purl across 28 sts of row 2 of chart, repeat from * 5 times more, k1. Continue as set, working 6 repeats of chart across the width of your bag body until all 52 rows of your charts have been worked, and ending with the right side facing for the next row.
Next row (RS): Purl. (Makes fold line). Beginning with a purl row, work in stockinette stitch for 5 rows, ending with a wrong side row. Cast off knitwise.

Bag Base
Using 4mm (US6) needles and background color, cast on 30 sts.
Beginning with a knit row, work in stockinette stitch for 70 rows.
Cast off knitwise.

Making Up
Block or press bag body and base as preferred, and sew in ends. With right sides together, stitch side seam of bag using the knit stitches at either end of the bag body as a seam allowance.

Keeping the right side of your work to the inside, pin the bag base to the bag body along the lower edge of the work, arranging the design so that the third and sixth flower are centered on the shorter edges of the base. Stitch bag base to bag body, and turn work right side out.

Carefully construct bag lining to match up to the shape you have constructed (see page 88).

Turn facings to the inside along garter stitch fold line, and slip-stitch facing to lining to secure.

Wrap bag handles with remaining background color yarn until they are covered, and secure. Stitch to inside facings.

LINING YOUR BAG
Measurements
A   Base Width
B   Bag Length
C   Bag Height (cast on edge to fold line)

Use your knitted pieces to measure the dimensions of A, B and C as listed above. Using the guide below, draw and cut out the cardboard lining pieces as detailed.

Punch holes as indicated.

Lay out the cardboard lining pieces as shown, and "stitch" together through the punched holes to form the lining structure.

Keeping the lining flat, spray with fabric adhesive and cover with a single piece of lining fabric. Trim, leaving an allowance of approx 2cm/¾in, and carefully turn the allowance to the wrong side.

Slide your lining into the project bag, fold over the facings and secure by slip stitching facings to the lining.

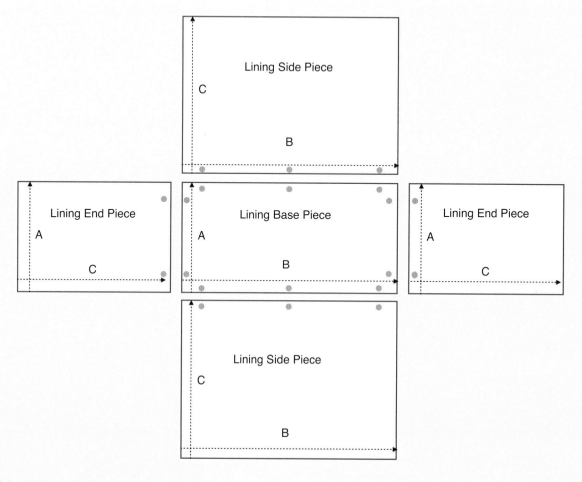

Chart

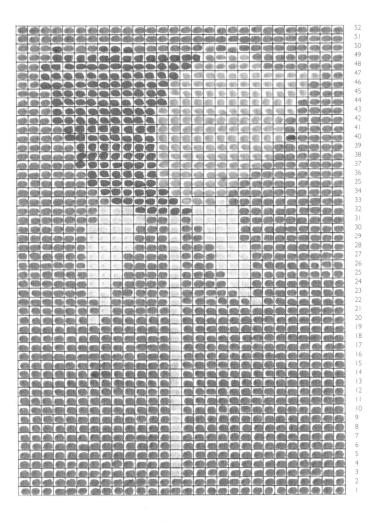

52
51
50
49
48
47
46
45
44
43
42
41
40
39
38
37
36
35
34
33
32
31
30
29
28
27
26
25
24
23
22
21
20
19
18
17
16
15
14
13
12
11
10
9
8
7
6
5
4
3
2
1

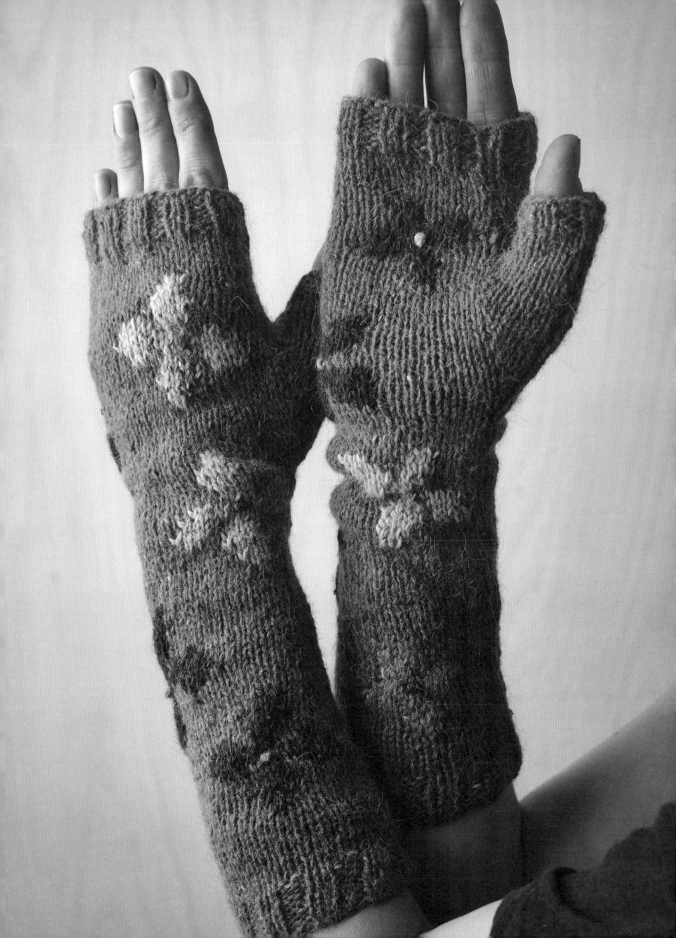

Wrist Warmers

Finished size: To fit average size woman's hand

Yarn: 175m/192yds × #3 Light Weight Yarn (shown in Rowan Felted Tweed in Watery 152). Short pieces of #3 Light Weight Yarn (shown in Rowan Felted Tweed: Rage 150, Bilberry 151, Ginger 154, Avocado 161, Frozen 185 and Tawny 186).

Needles: Pair of 3.75mm (US5) knitting needles
Pair of 4mm (US6) knitting needles

Extras:
2 stitch markers
Darning needle

Gauge: 22sts and 30 rows to 10cm/4in stockinette stitch on 4mm (US6) needles or needles required to obtain correct gauge.

Note: It is conventional to read the color chart from right to left for a right side row, and left to right for a wrong side row. In order to give you a mirror-image pair of wrist warmers, read the color chart from left to right for a right side row, and from right to left for a wrong side row when working the second wrist warmer.

Wrist Warmer (make 2)

Using 3.75mm (US5) needles, cast on 42 sts.
Rib row 1 (RS): K2, (p2, k2) to end.
Rib row 2 (WS): K1, p1, (k2, p2) to last 4 sts, k2, p1, k1.
Repeat rib rows 1 and 2 three times more, so that 8 rib rows have been worked in total.
Change to 4mm (US6) needles.
Beginning with a knit row, work the first 60 rows of chart in stockinette stitch, incorporating the intarsia motif where required.
Continue to knit the first and last stitch of every wrong side row.

Thumb Shaping

Using the chart as a guide, increase for thumb on either side of the center 40 sts as follows:
Row 1 (RS): K1, m1, pm, k to last st, pm, m1, k1. (44 sts).
Row 2 (WS): K1, purl to final stitch, slipping markers, k1.
Next row (RS): K to marker, m1, slip marker, pattern across center 40 sts of chart, slip marker, m1, k to end.
Next row (WS): K1, purl to last stitch, slipping markers, k1.

Repeat the last 2 rows, always referencing your color chart when working the 40 sts between the stitch markers, until you have 62 sts in total, ending with a wrong side row and removing the stitch markers on the final purl row.

Next row (RS): K10, turn and work 5 more rows of stockinette stitch on these 10 sts, beginning with a purl row.
Change to 3.75mm (US5) needles.
Rib row 1 (RS): K2, (p2, k2) to end.
Rib row 2 (WS): P2, (k2, p2) to end.
Repeat rib rows 1 and 2 once more.
Cast off in rib.

With right side facing and 4mm (US6) needles, rejoin yarn to remaining 52 sts and pattern to end, using your color chart as a guide.
Next row (WS): P10, turn and work 4 more rows of stockinette stitch on these 10 sts, beginning with a knit row.
Change to 3.75mm (US5) needles.
Rib row 1 (RS): K2, (p2, k2) to end.
Rib row 2 (WS): P2, (k2, p2) to end.
Repeat rib rows 1 and 2 once more.
Cast off in rib.

With wrong side facing and 4mm (US6) needles, rejoin yarn to center 42 sts. Work remaining 11 rows from chart.
Change to 3.75 mm (US5) needles and complete rib as follows:
Row 1 (RS): K2, (p2, k2) to end.
Row 2 (WS): P2, (k2, p2) to end.
Repeat rib rows 1 and 2 twice more so that 6 rib rows have been worked.
Cast off in rib.

Making Up

Block or press to size as preferred. With right sides together, fold wrist warmer in half down the mid line, so that the right sides of the thumb shaping are together.
Sew long side seam together.
Sew inner side seam together, leaving openings for the thumb and fingers.
Weave in ends.
Turn right side out.

Chart

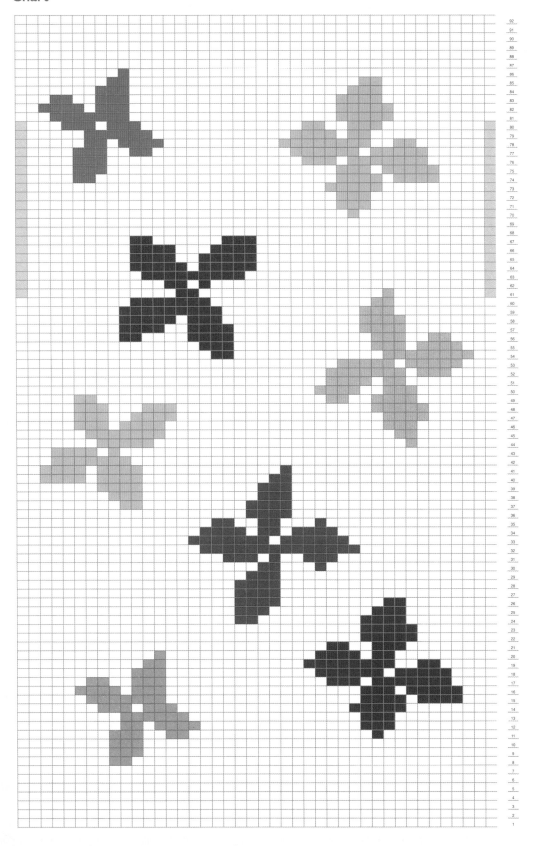

Wraparound Cushion

Finished size: Approx 45cm x 45cm / 17¾ x 17¾in ·

Yarn: 525m/575yds × #3 Light Weight Yarn (shown in Rowan Felted Tweed in Clay 177) for background color and short lengths of #3 Light Weight Yarn (shown in Rowan Felted Tweed) as required for intarsia detail.

Needles: Pair of 4mm (US6) knitting needles

Extras:
3 x 15mm/½in buttons
45cm/17¾in pillow
Darning needle

Gauge: 22 sts and 30 rows to 10cm/4in square measured over stockinette stitch using 4mm (US6) needles.

Notes: Beginning at row 1, your chart should be read from right to left for a right side (knit) row, and left to right for a wrong side (purl) row. I recommend knitting the first and last stitches of each wrong side row to give a visible seam allowance. This will help when sewing your cushion together.

Lower Back

Using 4mm (US 6) needles and background color (shown in Clay 177), cast on 102 sts.
Rib row 1 (RS): *K2, p2, repeat from * until 2 sts remain, k2.

Rib row 2 (WS): K1, p1, *k2, p2, repeat from * until 4 sts remain, k2, p1, k1.
Repeat rib rows 1 and 2 5 times more, so that 12 rows of rib have been worked.
Decrease row (RS): K50, k2tog, k50. (101 sts)
Beginning with a purl row, work 61 rows in stockinette stitch, ending with wrong side row.

Front

Working from row 1 of the chart and incorporating the intarsia design, continue as follows:
Row 1 (RS): Knit.
Row 2 (WS): Purl.
Continuing to work in stockinette stitch, you can now work across all 101 sts and 137 rows of your intarsia chart, ending with a right side row.

Upper Back

Beginning with a purl row, in background color work 62 rows in stockinette stitch, ending with a right side row.
Increase Row (WS): K1, p50, m1, p49, k1. (102 sts)
Working rib rows as set at beginning of lower back, work rib rows 3 times so that 6 rib rows have been worked.
Buttonhole Row (RS): Pattern 26, yo, p2tog, pattern 22, yo, p2tog, pattern 22, yo, p2tog, pattern to end.
Beginning with rib row 2, work 5 more rows of rib so that 12 rows have been worked in total, including the buttonhole row.
Cast off in rib.

Making Up

Block or press cushion as preferred, and sew in ends. With right sides together fold down the upper back at the fold line where the intarsia chart work finished. Fold up the lower back at the fold line where the intarsia chart work began.

Overlap the ribbed section, ensuring that the upper back rib with the buttonholes is positioned in between the cushion front and the plain rib.

This will ensure that your buttonholes are on the outside when you turn your cushion inside out.

Stitch both side seams of your cushion using the knit stitches along each edge as a seam allowance.

Turn your cushion cover right side out. Use the buttonholes as a guide for placing your buttons on the opposing rib edge. Insert cushion pad and close with buttons.

Chart

Key

☐ Light Gray (Clay 177)

■ Dark Green (Avocado 161)

■ Yellow (Mineral 181)

■ Gray (Carbon 159)

■ Aqua Blue (Watery 152)

■ Deep Red (Rage 150)

Shawl

Finished size: Approx 55cm wide (max) × 205cm / 21¾ × 80¾in long

Yarn: 1050m/1149yds #3 Light Weight Yarn (shown in Rowan Felted Tweed) for main body, plus short lengths as required for intarsia detail, embroidery, crochet edge and pom poms.

Needles: Pair of 4mm (US6) knitting needles, 4mm (USG/6) crochet hook

Extras:
35mm/¼in pom-pom maker
Darning needle

Gauge: 22 sts and 30 rows to 10cm/4in square measured over stockinette stitch using 4mm (US6) needles.

Note: Beginning at row 1, your charts should be read from right to left for a right side (knit) row, and left to right for a wrong side (purl) row.

Wrap Body

Using 4mm needles, cast on 8 sts.

Work scarf body increasing 2 stitches for every 6 row repeat as detailed below.
At the same time, incorporate intarsia petal motif as desired, keeping the motif outside the final 9 sts of a right side row to avoid working the motifs within the short rows.

Please note: The first time you work this 6 row repeat, you will be wrapping the final stitch in row 2.

Row 1: Knit until 7 sts remain on left hand needle, m1, k2, k2tog, yo, k3.
Row 2: K3, p5, wrap next st and turn.
Row 3: K3, k2tog, yo, k3.
Row 4: K3, p to last st, k1.
Row 5: Knit until 7 sts remain on left hand needle, m1, k2, k2tog, yo, k3.
Row 6: K3, p to last st, k1.
Repeat rows 1 to 6 55 times more until you have 120 sts on your needle, ending after working row 6.

Continue working scarf body without increasing as detailed below, continuing to incorporate intarsia motif as desired:

Row 1: Knit to last 5 sts, k2tog, yo, k3.
Row 2: K3, p5, wrap next st and turn.
Row 3: K3, k2tog, yo, k3.
Row 4: K3, p to last st, k1.
Row 5: Knit to last 5 sts, k2tog, yo, k3.
Row 6: K3, p to last st, k1.
Repeat rows 1 to 6 until work measures approx 130cm/51¼in from cast on edge, ending after row 6.
Now work scarf body decreasing 2 stitches for every 6 row repeat as detailed below, once again continuing to incorporate intarsia motif as desired.

Row 1: Knit until 8 sts remain on left hand needle, k2tog, k1, k2tog, yo, k3.

Row 2: K3, p5, wrap next st and turn.

Row 3: K3, k2tog, yo, k3.

Row 4: K3, p to last st, k1.

Row 5: Knit until 8 sts remain on left hand needle, k2tog, k1, k2tog, yo, k3.

Row 6: K3, p to last st, k1.

Repeat rows 1 to 6 fifty five times more until you have 8 sts remaining, ending after working row 6.

Please note: The last time you work this 6 row repeat, you will be wrapping the final stitch in row 2. Cast off knitwise.

Making Up

To add a crochet edge to your shawl:

Using a 4mm (USG/6) crochet hook starting at one end of your work, work a row of double crochet (US single crochet) into alternate rows, working up the curved side of your shawl.

Using split stitch, work free form loops around your design, using the photo on page 98 as a guide.

Make 4 small pom poms with matching scraps of yarn and fasten to the ends of the work with the tails of yarn left from finishing your pom pom.

Chart

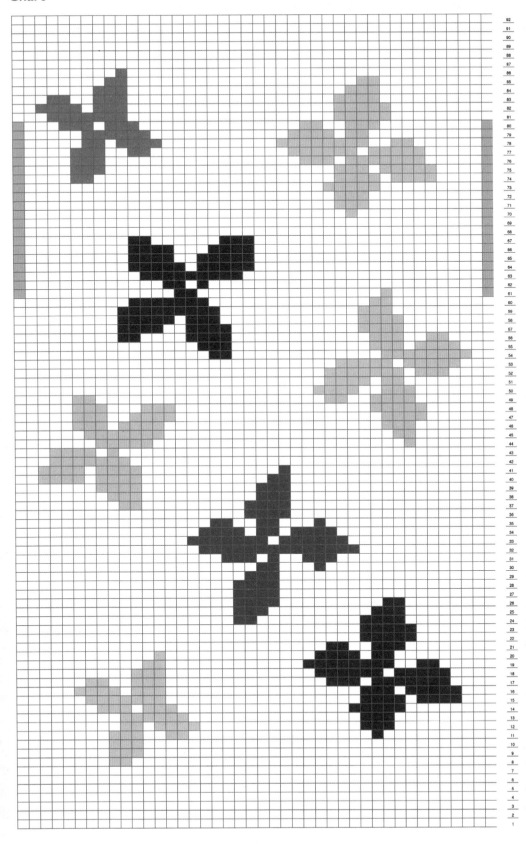

Abbreviations

Approx.	Approximately
Cm	Centimeters
In	Inches
K	Knit
K2tog	Knit 2 together
K2togtbl	Knit 2 together through back loop
M1	Make 1
MM	Milimeters
P	Purl
P2tog	Purl 2 together
P2togtbl	Purl 2 together through back loop
PM	Place marker
PSSO	Pass slipped stitch over
RS	Right side
Sl1	Slip 1
St st	Stockinette stitch
St/Sts	Stitch/Stitches
Sts	Stitches
WS	Wrong side
Yds	Yards
YO	Yarn over needle

Acknowledgments

This book is inspired by my love of the beautiful countryside that surrounds my home in Wales, and by the endless joys of working with yarn to celebrate the people, places and eye-catching details that make everyday life so special.

I would like to give special thanks to:
The Art Shop & Chapel for bringing truly artistic spaces to Abergavenny and for generously providing the creative setting for this book.
artshopandgallery.co.uk

Love Lily flowers, my local flower shop filled with exquisite floral bouquets, for providing the beautiful flowers in this book.
love-lily.com

The Wool Croft for supporting my Intarsia Design workshops and the inspiration that comes from Ginevra's gorgeous boutique wool shop.
thewoolcroft.co.uk

Georgie Park for happy days knitting and working together on the quilt.

Elizabeth of Mar and Marianne Hohendorf for reading drafts of my book with encouragement, enthusiasm and helpful suggestions.

Rowan Yarns for the rich palette of yarns provided for making this book and a wonderful world of yarn inspiration.
knitrowan.com

Jesse Wild for bringing everything together with his creative eye and beautiful photography.
jessewild.co.uk

And thank you to my fabulous publisher for allowing me the freedom to create this book, for their expertise and guidance, and for making the process of making a book so much fun!

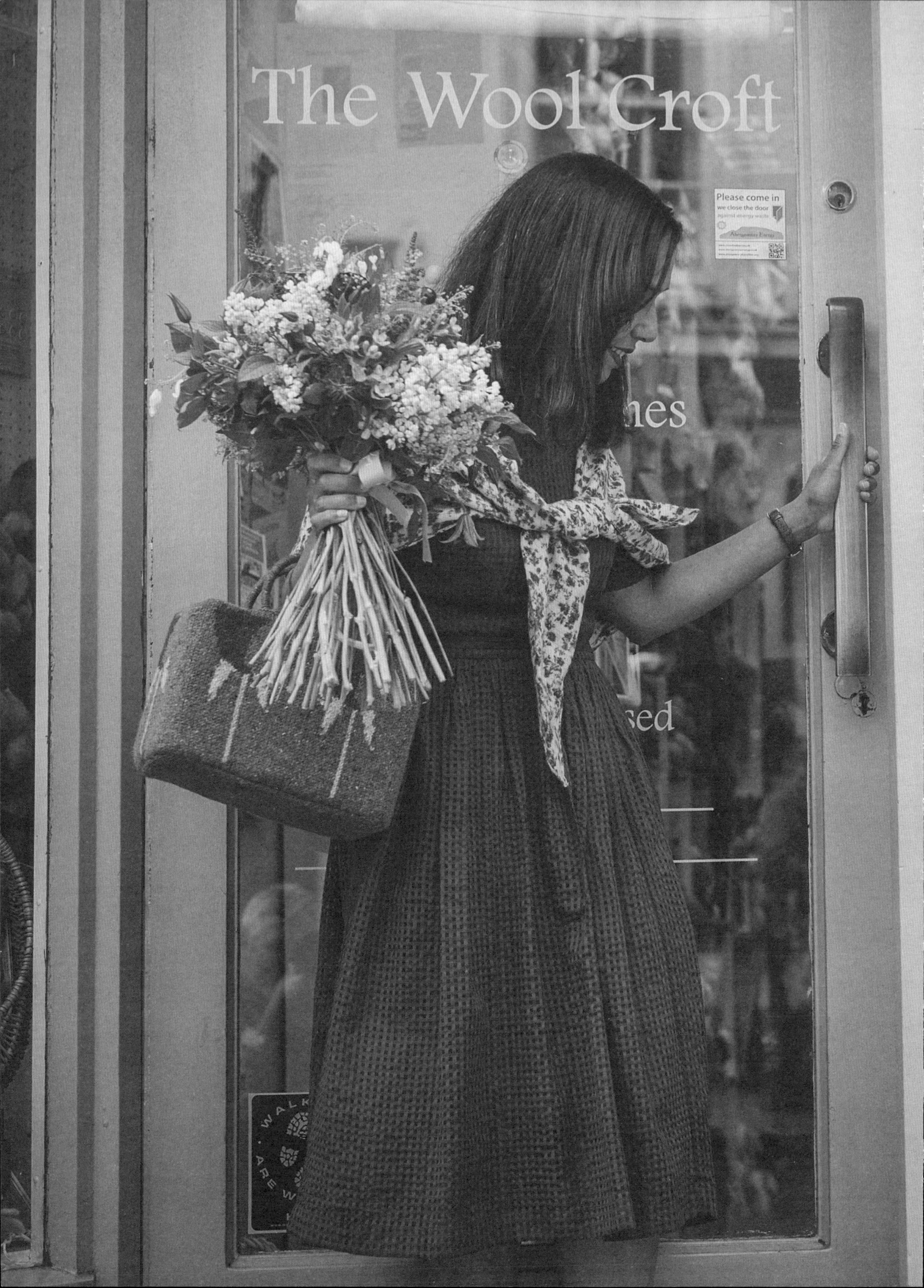
The Wool Croft
Please come in
we close the door

About The Author

Dee Hardwicke is an artist, designer and knitter with a passionate belief in creating beautiful and accessible pieces that bring color and joy to everyday life. Dee trained in the fine arts, and works from a studio in South Wales. She finds endless inspiration in the British countryside and always has a sketchbook to hand so that she can record the little details and colors that catch her eye throughout the seasons.

Dee's work encompasses everything from creating bespoke tiles and mosaics, to designing exclusive tableware collections for the National Trust. An enthusiastic knitter, Dee also loves translating her sketches into stunning knits and intarsia designs that will be treasured for years to come. Dee holds regular Intarsia Design workshops across the United Kingdom (please visit www.deehardwicke.co.uk for details).